D0745429

BEING AN ACTIVE CITIZEN
SERVING IN THE MILITARY

by Vincent Alexander

pogo

Ideas for Parents and Teachers

Pogo Books let children practice reading informational text while introducing them to nonfiction features such as headings, labels, sidebars, maps, and diagrams, as well as a table of contents, glossary, and index.

Carefully leveled text with a strong photo match offers early fluent readers the support they need to succeed.

Before Reading

- "Walk" through the book and point out the various nonfiction features. Ask the student what purpose each feature serves.
- Look at the glossary together. Read and discuss the words.

Read the Book

- Have the child read the book independently.
- Invite him or her to list questions that arise from reading.

After Reading

- Discuss the child's questions. Talk about how he or she might find answers to those questions.
- Prompt the child to think more. Ask: Do you know anyone who has served in the military? What was the experience like for him or her?

Pogo Books are published by Jump!
5357 Penn Avenue South
Minneapolis, MN 55419
www.jumplibrary.com

Library of Congress Cataloging-in-Publication Data

Names: Alexander, Vincent, author.
Title: Serving in the military / by Vincent Alexander.
Description: Pogo books. | Minneapolis : Jump!, Inc., [2019]
Series: Being an active citizen | Includes bibliographical references and index. | Audience: Ages 7-10.
Identifiers: LCCN 2018008747 (print)
LCCN 2018009885 (ebook)
ISBN 9781641280273 (e-book)
ISBN 9781641280259 (hardcover : alk. paper)
ISBN 9781641280266 (pbk. : alk. paper)
Subjects: LCSH: United States—Armed Forces
Juvenile literature.
Classification: LCC UA23 (ebook)
LCC UA23 .A548 2019 (print) | DDC 355.00973—dc23
LC record available at https://lccn.loc.gov/2018008747

Editor: Kristine Spanier
Book Designer: Molly Ballanger

Photo Credits: fstop123/iStock, cover; Aurora Photos/Alamy, 1; dcdebs/iStock, 3; Militarist/Shutterstock, 4; Tyler Stableford/Getty, 5; Ivan Cholakov/Shutterstock, 6-7; Lima Junior/Shutterstock, 7 (top left), (top middle), (top right), (bottom right); grzegorz knec/Alamy, 7 (bottom left); wingedwolf/iStock, 8-9; PJF Military Collection/Alamy, 10; John Moore/Getty, 11, 16; AJR_photo/Shutterstock, 12-13; Scott Olson/Getty, 14-15; 615 collection/Alamy, 17; Leonard Zhukovsky/Shutterstock, 18-19; michaeljung/Shutterstock, 20-21; stuar/Shutterstock, 23.

Printed in the United States of America at Corporate Graphics in North Mankato, Minnesota.

TABLE OF CONTENTS

CHAPTER 1

DEFENDING THE NATION

Defending the United States takes many people. How many? More than two million people!

A strong **military** helps to keep peace. It prevents others from attacking us. People who serve train to be ready. Every day they are on alert. They fly jets and command ships. They **patrol** the skies and seas.

There are five branches. All branches train for **combat**. What else? Peacekeeping. **Disaster** assistance. And human **welfare** tasks.

U.S. COAST GUARD

TAKE A LOOK!

Each branch has different duties. What are they?

U.S. AIR FORCE

Provides rapid air and space response and defense all around the world. Participates in peacekeeping, humanitarian, and evacuation missions.

U.S. ARMY

Provides land defense and combat power. Defends the United States, its territories, and its properties all around the world.

U.S. COAST GUARD

Provides law enforcement, port security, and environmental disaster response. Performs rescues on the nation's waters and maintains waterways.

U.S. MARINE CORPS

Provides first response for missions on land, at sea, and in the air. Trained and equipped to answer threats all around the world.

U.S. NAVY

Provides peace and stability for travel and trade in the world's oceans. Performs sea-based missions with some by land and air.

veterans

PATROL

Service members are divided into three groups. Active duty are people who are currently serving full-time. The Reserve and National Guard members are trained. They serve when needed. Veterans are people who are no longer serving. People do not have to see combat to be veterans.

DID YOU KNOW?

Different branches have their own names for the people who serve. The Air Force has airmen. The Army has soldiers. The Coast Guard has coast guardsmen. The Marine Corps has marines. The Navy has sailors.

CHAPTER 2

LIFE IN THE MILITARY

Most service members are **enlisted**. With time and hard work, they rise to higher **ranks**. They may get leadership roles. They may become officers.

officer

enlisted

U.S. NAVY

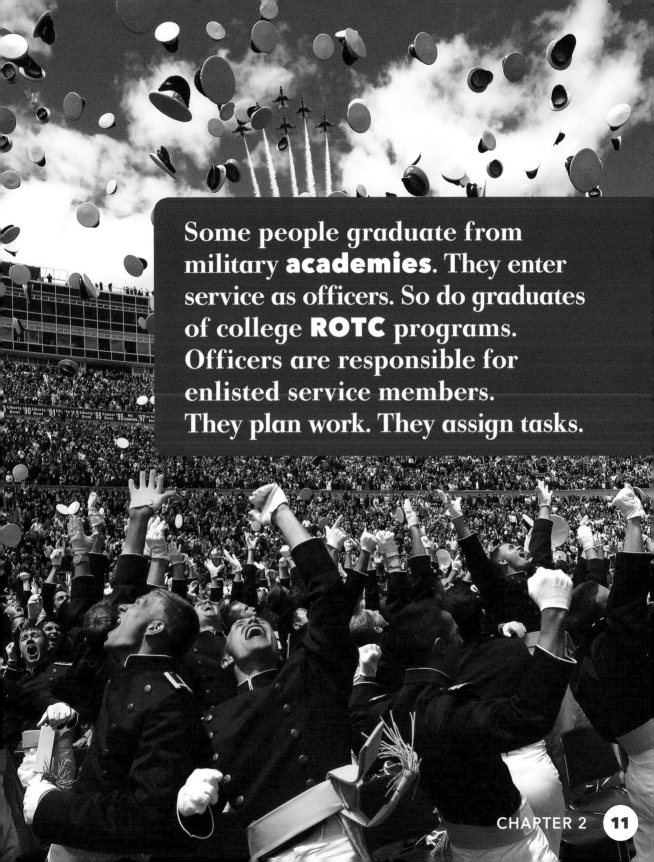

Some people graduate from military **academies**. They enter service as officers. So do graduates of college **ROTC** programs. Officers are responsible for enlisted service members. They plan work. They assign tasks.

Some service members may never see combat. They may work as doctors. Nurses. Carpenters. Truck drivers. Cooks. Plumbers. Even illustrators!

WHAT DO YOU THINK?

Many kinds of jobs are offered in the armed forces. There are even jobs for people who play instruments. What kind of job would you want?

What are the **benefits** of serving? World travel. Money for education. New skills to use later to earn money. Medical care. People may spend their entire **careers** in the military.

Serving is serious. The training is hard. Combat is dangerous. Some may need to leave their families for long periods. They may have trouble adjusting after returning. But serving is important to our nation.

CHAPTER 3

ACTIVE CITIZENS

Why do people serve?
They want to help
keep our country safe.
It is one way to be
an active citizen.

They are people who want to make
the world better. Some are active
in their own states. Others are
active far from home.

People who serve learn responsibility. Respect. They have courage and honor. They take **pride** in serving their country. These are the qualities of an active citizen.

Thank the service members you see. Be kind to people who have family members serving away from home. **Donating** items to veterans' hospitals makes a difference, too. Supporting service members is another way to be an active citizen.

WHAT DO YOU THINK?

The armed forces help defend us. But how can we help prevent war? How can we work for peace?

ACTIVITIES & TOOLS

MAKE CARE PACKAGES

People serving might be far from home. Sometimes they do not have much contact with the outside world. You can support them! Collect items to send in care packages. These packages remind them that there are people who appreciate the work that they do.

❶ Gather items that service members need. Some ideas are:
- AA and AAA batteries
- hand sanitizer
- lip balm, toothpaste, cough drops
- magazines, newspapers, books
- nonperishable food items like trail mix and jerky
- socks (black, brown, green, or tan)
- tissue
- toiletries (travel size)

❷ Write a short letter or draw a picture to include with your package. Make sure to thank the recipient for his or her service. Decorate your box, address the label carefully, and bring it to the post office.

❸ If you don't know anyone personally, you can contact www.operationgratitude.com. This organization will ship your items to troops who need them.

academies: Special universities that teach military subjects.

benefits: Valuable things that come with a job in addition to pay.

careers: The work or the series of jobs that people have.

combat: Fighting between nations or with terrorist organizations.

disaster: An event that causes great damage, loss, or suffering.

donating: Giving something to a charity or a cause.

enlisted: People who are active members of the military who are not officers.

military: The armed forces of a country.

patrol: To travel around an area to watch or protect it.

pride: A feeling of satisfaction in something that you or someone else has achieved.

ranks: Official job levels or positions.

ROTC: Reserve Officer Training Corps, a college program that prepares people to become officers in the military.

welfare: Aid for those in need.

INDEX

TO LEARN MORE

Learning more is as easy as 1, 2, 3.

1) Go to www.factsurfer.com

2) Enter "servinginthemilitary" into the search box.

3) Click the "Surf" button to see a list of websites.

With factsurfer, finding more information is just a click away.